In Vino Veritas
Pellucid Press, 2017

Contents

Introduction		3
Lesson 1:	Celebration	5
Lesson 2:	*Terroir*	12
Lesson 3:	Connection	20
Lesson 4:	Time	26
Lesson 5:	Pruning	34
Lesson 6:	Harvest	43
Lesson 7:	Filling	54
Lesson 8:	Transmission	64
Lesson 9:	Transformation	73
Lesson 10:	Pouring	84
Epilogue		92
Sur Lie		96

Acknowledgments

I gratefully wish to thank the following people:

1. My wife Sylvia who helped inspire this study at the *Gasthaus Weingut Stahl*, Oberwesel, Germany, along with friends in France, Lebanon, Israel, Argentina, South Africa, California, and of course Virginia.

2. The owners of Cana Vineyards and Winery of Middleburg, Virginia, who kindly allowed me to photograph their beautiful vineyards. All images in this book are from their property or reproduced from Pixabay.com.

3. The staff and congregation of Providence Baptist Church, McLean, Virginia whose encouragement and feedback provided fertile soil for this book to grow.

May God richly bless each of you.

INTRODUCTION

Jesus taught truth through the common realities of the world in which he and his listeners lived. He illustrated principles often overlooked in the daily life of a 1st century eastern Roman province. A carpenter who lived with fishermen and tax collectors, Jesus spoke to men, women and children who related to fish, bread, and sheep.

And wine. Hebrew scriptures often mention wine gladdening the heart and accompanying ritual observances. In both the Old and New Testament, writers describe healthy effects in moderation but warn against overconsumption – a reminder of the importance of balance in life. In the Gospel of John, Jesus begins and ends his ministry with wine. It is is a complex substance, the artful marriage of God's creation with our interventions, studied over millenia.

Several points in this book come from France. French viticulture began several centuries before Christ with Greek settlers in Marseille. The Gauls advanced winemaking and pruning techniques and in the Middle Ages, French monks maintained these skills for profit as well for the Eucharist. Wine crosses cultures, influencing them and being influenced in return.

Good wine expresses clarity and complexity with relatively few ingredients. Fermentation and aging allow the right chemicals to interact to produce a pleasant overall effect. Similarly, this study is dependent on your interaction with each scripture and lesson for maximum benefit. Interactive participation among study group members is the key to not only effectively exploring spiritual truths, but also to the equally important task of building a community of seekers.

In short, wine production is dynamic, just as God wishes our life to be with Him. 17th century British theologians asserted that chief end of humanity is to "glorify God and enjoy Him forever." Over the following ten chapters, enjoy the richness of God. As the Jewish toast says, *L'Chayim*! -- to life!

– I –

CELEBRATION

John 2: 2-10

On the third day there was a wedding in Cana of Galilee, and the mother of Jesus was there; and both Jesus and His disciples were invited to the wedding. When the wine ran out, the mother of Jesus said to Him, "They have no wine." And Jesus said to her, "Woman, what does that have to do with us? My hour has not yet come." His mother said to the servants, "Whatever He says to you, do it." Now there were six stone waterpots set there for the Jewish custom of purification, containing twenty or thirty gallons each. Jesus said to them, "Fill the waterpots with water." So they filled them up to the brim. And He said to them, "Draw some out now and take it to the headwaiter." So they took it to him.

When the headwaiter tasted the water which had become wine, and did not know where it came from (but the servants who had drawn the water knew), the headwaiter called the bridegroom, and said to him,"Every man serves the good wine first, and when the people have drunk freely, then he serves the poorer wine; but you have kept the good wine until now."

§

They were celebrating a beginning, the joining of lives.

From then on, nothing would be the same.

A young guest stands in the corner. His own parents' ceremony decades before was tainted by scandal and held without fanfare, meager in comparison. He had no distinctive appearance, but his neighbors regarded him well as one who labored diligently to help his father's carpentry trade. The man had a determined spirit – he'd just arrived from a 70-mile hike from the south. He could have justifiably spent the day resting, but he came to the wedding anyway. Perhaps to please his parents, perhaps to enjoy a change in scenery with his closest friends whom he'd brought along.

His mother approaches, hurried and anxious. Was there trouble? Was someone ill? Brows furrowed, she furtively shares they have no wine. We can almost hear him sigh. He raises his shoulders – "what does that have to do with me?" He thinks about what he had planned for his for his own life – "my time hasn't come."

Then, despite the shame of his parents' awkward wedding, despite his own plans and desires, he walks over to six stone jars, each almost large enough for 30 gallons. He knows their purpose. From time spent in the Temple, he recognized their contents were usually reserved for purification rites, another ceremony for another type of beginning. He pauses, then smiles and says to the servants "fill these with water."

Ordinary, taken for granted, life-sustaining water. At this stranger's command, they fill them to the brim and without looking inside, he orders they be taken directly to the feast master. The master tastes, then his face widens into a broad smile and he calls the groom to commend him for keeping the best for last.

He didn't drink water, but wine.

And so Jesus Christ unassumingly, unexpectedly entered public life. With an over-the-top act of extravagance and art, content to let its beauty enhance the joy of those around him, unembellished with words, unadorned with teaching.

Thoughts for sharing:

1. We don't know exactly why Jesus walked all the way from Bethany beyond the Jordan to Galilee, but he did it in an astonishingly short period, testifying to a resolute personality. Rather than nap in the next day, he participated in a family friend's celebration. How do we interact with others? Do we honor our commitments? Do we show genuine interest in others' lives? Do we share in our neighbors' joys and sorrows?

   Do we view life and God's gifts as reasons for celebrations? Do you think that doing so honors God? Does He celebrate? Business leader Max Depree asserts one of the signals of an organization's deterioration is "no longer having time for celebration." Christ could have easily said it wasn't his responsibility, that planners lacked foresight, or that additional wine would be a waste. But he didn't. Why do you think not?

2. Jesus was not planning to begin his ministry, yet responded to the request for assistance from one he loved. How do we show extravagant love? From where does this love come? How do we stay responsive to others' needs? Are we willing to change our own plans?

3. The wedding host is astounded that the best wine is served last. How should we consider the quality of the work and service we do, even in seemingly unimportant areas? Why?

4. There were doubtlessly plenty of people with illness and serious problems in the community where Jesus visited, yet we only read of Jesus providing fine wine at a party there. In John 12 we read about Mary pouring expensive perfume on Jesus' feet, offending Judas who used the disciples' finances for his own gain. Are Christians ever justified in lavish or more-than-essential expenses? Why or why not?

5. Sommeliers still debate what makes a great wine. Data demonstrate several foibles of human nature; reputation and limited supply often impress us more than genuinely distinguishable personal taste profiles. Still, the qualities most sought after are worth us considering as Christians. *La Revue du Vin de France* uses a concise 20 point scale. 11 or fewer points is considered mediocre: such wines lack three things – concentration, maturity, and balance. Conversely, exceptional wines are noted for their elegance, complexity, and strength.

The rarified few that achieve 20 authentically express their *terroir* and simultaneously offer complexity and elegance. They also mature well, improving with time.

What do you think characterizes an excellent follower of Christ? Do any of the adjectives above? Which ones and why? What other words can you think of to describe those who follow Christ well?

6. St. Francis of Assisi is frequently misquoted as saying, "preach the gospel and use words if necessary." In reality, he was a very vocal preacher. Jesus did not use this opportunity to teach with words. Why do you think he didn't?

– 2 –

TERROIR

Luke 8:4-8, 11-15

When a large crowd was coming together, and those from the various cities were journeying to Him, He spoke by way of a parable: "The sower went out to sow his seed; and as he sowed, some fell beside the road, and it was trampled under foot and the birds of the air ate it up. Other seed fell on rocky soil, and as soon as it grew up, it withered away, because it had no moisture. Other seed fell among the thorns; and the thorns grew up with it and choked it out. Other seed fell into the good soil, and grew up, and produced a crop a hundred times as great." As He said these things, He would call out, "He who has ears to hear, let him hear."

"Now the parable is this: the seed is the word of God. Those beside the road are those who have heard; then the devil

comes and takes away the word from their heart, so that they will not believe and be saved. Those on the rocky soil are those who, when they hear, receive the word with joy; and these have no firm root; [c]they believe for a while, and in time of temptation fall away. The seed which fell among the thorns, these are the ones who have heard, and as they go on their way they are choked with worries and riches and pleasures of this life, and bring no fruit to maturity. But the seed in the good soil, these are the ones who have heard the word in an honest and good heart, and hold it fast, and bear fruit with perseverance."

§

In the last chapter we saw Jesus make a superior wine out of plain water. The Lord asks us to be fruitful as well; how do we responde to him to produce our very best? We start where human winemakers begin -- with the grapes. Excellent wine starts with grapes selected to match the local climate and have the potential to deliver richness and complexity of flavor. It can be intimidating for us to aspire to yield such quality. Consider Mother Teresa's perspective, however: "God has not called me to be successful; he has called me to be faithful." We're to respond in faith, trusting God that our best is adequate, regardless how it appears to others.

In humility we remember Christ's words, "you did not choose me, but I chose you..." (John 15:16a). Each vintner knows the end results sought and how to achieve them. The disciples weren't chosen for their oratory skills, social standing, or financial resources – their only obvious requirement was willingness to follow Christ wherever it took them.

Many wine experts agree with the philosophy that the best wine is grown and consumed locally, regardless of varietal or style. In the same way, we glorify God when we trust he can use and transform us with all our unique quirks and limitations for His variety of purposes. It would be a boring world with only Chardonnay and only one type of Christian.

Once chosen and committed we begin to grow. Winemakers know two fundamental things about grapes – they all need lots of sun, and they're all rooted. That is, they have a universal need for the energy from a star millions of miles away, but they can only grow rooted in very local conditions. They each develop at a unique latitude and longitude. They're exposed to breezes from a specfic direction and sun from a circumscribed set of angles. They're rooted in a soil with shaping characteristics like acidity and drainage ability. Burgundian monks advanced this concept the French call *terroir*.

Some take a narrow view of *terroir*, considering just the chemical or geological properties of a plot of land. In reality, it's a broader perspective that embraces the effects of the entire local *milieu*. Latitude and altitude influence temperature swings. Topography affects the breeze patterns and the frost risk that may vary within the same vineyard. Aspect refers to the direction of the land toward or away from the sun. The plot's slope contributes to the aspect, but just as importantly to the drainage.

As one wine writer observed, "one of the wonderful mysteries of growing wine grapes is trying to understand the concept of *terroir*, the aromas and flavors that a vineyard site gives to the wine. Your site will have its own *terroir*, but you cannot know what those flavors will be until you start making wine from your own grapes."*

Similarly, we are each called to use our unique resources and talents for the Lord, something no one else can do. This is true regardless how we consider our adequacy. If the average person on the street were asked to describe the best soil for growing grapes, he or she would likely advocate for the richest, most fertile material. Maximize nutrients and water, and supply in overabundance all the ingredients a vine can absorb. In reality, you probably *would* get luxuriant, wonderfully verdant vines. But terrible wine.

* Law, J, *The Backyard Vintner*, Quarry Books, Gloucester, MA, 2005

Likely in contrast to our expectations, poor, depleted soil is actually *desirable* for wine. Rich soil tends to produce too many shoots and grapes that dilute flavor. Excess nutrients are shunted to the leaves, creating a beautiful canopy that comfortably shades insipid grapes. The most desired fruit grows in impoverished soil that forces vines to slowly concentrate their essence. Meager soil disciplines the plant to produce less showy vegetation and fewer but more satisfying grapes.

It's a similar paradox with water. Drainage is critical. Viticulturalists say "grapes hate wet feet," and when they talk about soil -- clay, silt, sand, and rocks – they're really communicating how much water is retained. Too much moisture encourages fungus growth that harms the plant's foundation.

Like the master vintner, God knows two things about us: we need lots of exposure to his Son, and each of us rooted in unique circumstances that he understands. And as with wine grapes, challenging soil is indispensable for our spiritual growth. We should remember that in a world where success is often measured differently than the God does. However, it's a far cry from Nietzsche's criticism of religion which asserts that spirituality sadistically dampens life's natural healthy tendencies. The Bible doesn't advocate denial for denial's sake, but for a greater, more enduring satisfaction.

As a final note on *terroir*, observe that in the parable of the sower the message isn't just about the soil, but also of the nearby plants and animals. We have the ability to determine part of our own environment and cultivate healthy, inspiring relationships (Proverbs 27:17, I Thessalonians 5:11).

Above all, it helps in difficult times to remember that we are called to "bear fruit with perseverance." Difficult circumstances aren't necessarily always ordained by God, but if we let Him, He can use those times to mature us and grow rich fruit that blesses others.

Thoughts for sharing:

1. An otherwise-unidentified man, Agur, asks God in Proverbs 30 for freedom from both poverty and riches so that he might not sin in human weakness. Paul emphasizes his dependence on God to meet such challenges in Philippians 4:13: "I know how to get along with humble means, and I also know how to live in prosperity; in any and every circumstance I have learned the secret of being filled and going hungry, both of having abundance and suffering need. I can do all things through Him who strengthens me."

In 2 Corinthians 12:9-11, Paul once again relates how he overcome temptations in suffering: *"And He has said to me, "My grace is sufficient for you, for power is perfected in weakness." Most gladly, therefore, I will rather boast about my weaknesses, so that the power of Christ may dwell in me. Therefore I am well content with weaknesses, with insults, with distresses, with persecutions, with difficulties, for Christ's sake; for when I am weak, then I am strong."*

What do you think Paul means? Are there any areas in your life in which you feel unfulfilled, unsatisfied, or otherwise lacking? Do you think God can help? How?

2. In 2 Corinthians 1:4-5, Paul thanks God who "who comforts us in all our affliction so that we will be able to comfort those who are in any affliction with the comfort with which we ourselves are comforted by God." Have you ever gone through a difficult situation and later been

uniquely able to help someone else because of your experience?

3. Think of two or three periods in life when you grew spiritually. Did any of them involve hardship, frustration, or limitation?

4. Are there difficult situations you or others close to you are currently facing? How do you think God can bring good out it?

5. Many leadership books assert you can find your niche not by looking at desires or interests but by one's history and circumstances. Reflect on your life, your successes, failures, youth, talents, etc. Can you see how God used one stage of your life (perhaps one you initially regarded as a failure or undesired) to prepare you for a later one? Can you see a pattern that suggests how God might call you in the future?

6. Wine grapes grow best in well-drained soil as roots in a wet, stagnant environment rapidly rot. The water needs to be quickly absorbed and the excess distributed rather than just soak the earth. In the Christian life, what can occur if we are blessed in receiving, but don't share that with others? Is the joy of receiving gifts diminished, unaffected, or enhanced in sharing with others? Can you think of examples?

CONNECTION

John 15:5, 12-15

I am the vine; you are the branches. If you remain in me and I in you, you will bear much fruit; apart from me you can do nothing.

This is My commandment, that you love one another, just as I have loved you. Greater love has no one than this, that one lay down his life for his friends. You are My friends if you do what I command you. No longer do I call you slaves, for the slave does not know what his master is doing; but I have called you friends, for all things that I have heard from My Father I have made known to you.

§

It wasn't pleasant for the disciples in the upper room. After pulling them away from their comfortable lives and uprooting their plans, Jesus says he will be leaving them. John records two chapters earlier, "Jesus knew that he hour had come for him to leave... Having loved his own who were in the world, he loved them to the end."

It wasn't a time for sentimentality. Golgotha was a short steep walk away. Some ask him to at least show them God to reassure them. He says he already has. Others complain they wouldn't know how to follow him. He says they already know the way. To those frettting around the table, he says they would do even more than he had. More than the One who had walked on water, raised the dead, and calmed the sea. The one thing he guarantees to leave them is peace, yet they don't feel it.

To his anxious followers, he speaks frankly but in love. "I am the true vine, and my Father is the gardener. He cuts off every branch that bears no fruit." Harsh. But he continues with another promise: *if* they remain in him, they *will* bear fruit for the Father's glory. The message is clear – our purpose and fulfillment is found in yielding fruit. Impossible to do without him living in us. Impossible *not* to do when he lives in us – maybe not as much as we'd like to imagine every day, but certainly in God's seasons for us.

21

It wasn't the first time Christ offered them a blessing with a condition. In John 8:32, Jesus says *"the truth shall set you free."* This maxim is often quoted even today, but without the qualification from the preceding verse: *"... Jesus said 'if you hold to my teaching, you really are my disciples. Then you will know the truth, and the truth shall set you free."* A virtuous circle begins when faithfulness in action leads to increased insight and faith that leads us to further service.

The healthy Christian life, like any other, implies growth. Feeding and exercise are needed to avoid atrophy and stiffness. Romans 12:2 adjures us *"do not be conformed to this world, but be transformed by the renewing of your mind."* Philippians 4:8-9 tells us how: *"... whatever is true, whatever is noble, whatever is right, whatever is lovely, whatever is admirable – if anything is excellent or praiseworthy – think about these things."* II Peter 1:5-8 adds: *"For this very reason, make every effort to add to your faith goodness; and to goodness, knowledge; and to knowledge, self-control; and to self-control, perseverance; and to perseverance, godliness; and to godliness, mutual affection; and to mutual affection, love. For if you possess these qualities in increasing measure, they will keep you from being ineffective..."*

In the mystery of salvation, we depend on God's grace and guidance, but we also must act to yield the unique gifts He's destined for us to offer the world that He loves (Ephesians 2:10).

As we take hold of the divine life, we will at times find it contrary to our inclinations. Left to our own intuition and tendencies, we'll never get rooted. In the 1800's, winemakers introduced European varietals to California but their stock was decimated by the root louse *Phylloxera*. They discovered that grafting European vines onto native roots provided resilience, allowing them to produce healthy fruit with a unique blend of taste -- part host, part graft. As Jesus prepares his disciples for an unwelcome transition, he informs them their status has changed, from servants to chosen friends who know the Father's business and can bear fruit. They'd been *grafted*.

Colossians 3:3 tells us our lives are now hidden with Christ. We also are grafted and to grow we must depend on him. Our natural roots must die daily for God's love and power to flow. Only then can we live out the command "love each other as I have loved you." Thanks to our Lord for helping us remain in Him!

Thoughts for sharing:

1. If Christ is the true vine, what type of fruit should Christians bear? Is all fruit the same? Should it be? What makes the difference?

2. Read I Corinthians 3:6-8. Do you think you will always see the fruit that you've contributed to? If not, how does your confidence in God provide endurance to remain faithful? Personal fruit (see Galatians 5:22-23) may be appreciated right away. Investments we make in others (see Matthew 25:22-23, 31-40) may not be apparent until after this life. Can the presence or absence of short-term fruit help us assess if we're on track with long-term goals?

3. According to Jesus what _will_ happen if we remain in Him? How do we remain in Christ?

4. Read Psalm 127:1-2. Do you think Jesus was serious or exaggerating when he said without him we can do nothing? Why? If you have time, compare with the parable of the rich young ruler (Matthew 19:16-22).

5. Read John 13:1 (if possible in your group, from both NIV and KJV). Jesus loved his friends to the end, ultimately dying for them. During his time on earth, how else did he express his love for them? What does it mean to be called friend according to Jesus?

6. Read verse 16. Who chose whom? Is that an important distinction? Why or why not?

7. According to Jesus in that same verse, his disciples were chosen and appointed for what? What do you think God has called you to do? If you had to write a one-sentence summary of your life's purpose, what would it say? Why?

– 4 –

TIME

John 15: 8-12, 16-17

My Father is glorified by this, that you bear much fruit, and so prove to be My disciples. Just as the Father has loved Me, I have also loved you; abide in My love. If you keep My commandments, you will abide in My love; just as I have kept My Father's commandments and abide in His love. These things I have spoken to you so that My joy may be in you, and that your joy may be made full. This I command you, that you love each other as I have loved you.

You did not choose Me but I chose you, and appointed you that you would go and bear fruit, and that your fruit would remain, so that whatever you ask of the Father in My name

He may give to you. This I command you, that you love one another.

§

While living in Northern California many years ago, I spent an afternoon walking among the giant sequoias in Yosemite National Park. They dwarfed the other trees and bushes that were themselves far taller than me. I marveled how they stood apart from the life around them, as if they belonged on a different planet. These behemoths shared the same soil, temperature range, humidity, and to varying degrees, sun exposure as all the other plants, yet they were in a class all their own. In fact, one of them has been identified as the *largest living organism in the world*, over 30 stories tall, more than 100 feet wide, and almost 3 million pounds in weight! With all the same resources as their neighbors, these behemoths stand apart because of just two factors: DNA and time.

They are wired to relentlessly grow skywards to gain sun exposure and once rewarded with ample light, begin to thicken and add mass for a long, long, long time. Under optimal conditions, their growth can accelerate for a thousand years, and some may survive up to three millennia. They're in no rush to sprout and then step aside after a few decades or centuries like most trees – they're there for the long haul and make the most of it.

Time is also important for wine. Even with the best DNA, soil, microclimate and nurturing, vines require a minimum longevity to produce good quality fruit. For the first three years of a vine's life, the fruit is thrown away without even sampling a taste. Those early grapes are removed so the plant can invest its resources in growing a solid trunk. The "third leaf" (first crop of the third year) may be passable, but generally 5-6 years are needed to get quality fruit. Even at two decades (sometimes at a *century!*), when the plant slows down and produces fewer grapes, the quality frequently continues to improve.[*]

The spiritual life can't be rushed either. In God's economy, some things simply take a while to happen. No shortcuts. In contrast to today's media that emphasizes youth and novelty, maturity – typically gained by persistence and perseverance – is valued throughout the Bible. Jesus gradually grew in stature and favor with man and God, preparing three decades for three years of teaching, service, and sacrifice. As we recall from Chapter 1, he even protested when his mother first called him into the public sphere.

[*] Nickles, J, *Certified Specialist of Wine Study Guide 2015*, Society of Wine Educators, Washington D.C., 2015

Paul also apparently needed a lengthy time to prepare, despite his rigorous training in Judaism and dramatic encounter with Christ. After conversion, he spent three years in Arabia and Damascus before beginning his ministry in Jerusalem and beyond. (Galatians 1:15-18)

Three times in the passage above, Jesus emphasizes "abiding" – both his and his disciples'. The Greek word he uses, *ménō*, means "to stay, continue, dwell, or endure in a place, state, relation, or expectancy." *(Strong's Concordance* 3306). In short, to abide is to remain steadfast over time. For the Christian, that means to persistently, perseveringly obey and love. With the goal in mind, like an upward-reaching sequoia or vineyard patiently tended over decades, Paul encourages his friends. Despite aging, they're getting better, more like the Lord – "So we do not lose heart. Though our outer self is wasting away, our inner self is being renewed day by day... for the things we see are transient, but the things that are unseen are eternal" (2 Corinthians 4:16, 18b)

The other temporal topic Christ addresses here is sustainability. His Father isn't just interested in fruit, but fruit that will *remain*. An African proverb counsels, "if you want something done fast, do it yourself. If you want it to last, do it with others." It's true with wine as well -- the best structured reds age gracefully for years in barrels that lend additional flavors, enriching the complexity and taste as molecules mysteriously interact, becoming a product far richer than the sum of its parts.

It's even truer in the Church – we need each other. God has demonstrated incredible humility in establishing us as His body on earth. We are intended and commanded to serve each other and our Lord in a loving community that appreciates each element. It's not surprising then that Jesus emphasizes prayers are most readily received wherever "two or more are gathered in [His] name."

I should mention one additional advantage these towering plants have. To gain enough moisture near the top of their canopies, mature trees develop additional roots in the air. Mature Christians likewise develop deep roots in the Lord and also in a community of believers to encourage and support them as they grow.

During that trip to Yosemite two decades ago, I was struggling to choose between an excellent but long, arduous path and a shorter but less versatile one. As I considered the magnificent sequoias that patiently grew over hundreds of years, the decision became easy. I've never regretted my choice and thank God for that wisdom.

Thoughts for sharing:

1. How do we demonstrate we are true disciples?

2. How do we abide in Christ's love?

3. What is Jesus' commandment? What are two explicit reasons He gave us that commandment?

4. What are some practical ways we can demonstrate the kind of love he commands?

5. Paul Brand, a missionary surgeon who wrote numerous medical and spiritual books once said, "Living with God is like being in a boat. You may at times feel you're being prepared for one destination, and then you arrive at a different one that's ultimately better. Your responsibility is to allow God to turn the rudder and keep rowing wherever he's pointing." In other words, at every juncture in our lives, we're to work at whatever is in front of us with all our heart. (Colossians 3:23)

Besides being faithful to your daily responsibilities, what do you do when you feel your direction is on hold? What did Jesus' followers do?

6. Can you think of a time when you felt God initially denied or delayed a situation, and then brought a you to a better one? Are there currently areas in your life which

you feel are "on hold," unresolved, or unfulfilled? How can you more completely trust God in those issues?

6. A Russian proverb says, "it's never too late to turn back from going down the wrong road." Another common adage advises, "the first thing to do when you've dug yourself into a hole is stop digging." Have you ever regretted rushing into a situation? Have you ever experienced God redeeming a bad or difficult situation you've created? What did you learn from that experience?

7. John 15:16 shares God chose you so that you would *"bear fruit, and that your fruit would remain."* (NIV alternately translates as, *"fruit that will last."*) What's the difference between all fruit, and that which will last? What do you have to do (or *not* do) to produce the latter? Does the (possibly African) proverb "if you want to go fast, walk alone; if you want to go far, go together" have any bearing? How?

8. What would you do for God if you knew you would succeed? What's holding you back? Why not start today?

– 5 –

PRUNING

John 15:1-2

I am the true vine, and My Father is the vinedresser. Every branch in Me that does not bear fruit, He takes away; and every branch that bears fruit, prunes it so that it may bear more fruit.

§

Grape vines are maintained to bear fruit, and they need generous exposure to the sun to do so. For Northern Hemisphere vineyards, the orientation should generally be toward the south to maximize exposure to the sun. Ideally, the land is sloped to further angle toward the source of life. The smart master places the rows just far enough apart to avoid shading from adjacent rows that rob plants of sunlight.

After selecting the best grape for the climate, picking the right plot of terrain, and planting the vines with the right spacing and alignment, the nearly omnipotent winemaker then has to wait for the vine to respond.

He or she knows that, left to itself, the vine will shunt resources to fruitless areas instead of nourishing the best possible grapes. So as the vine develops, the master uses a variety of means to enrich the quality of the grape. He or she can manage the soil richness and water access. Considerable thought is put into arranging the layout of the vines, including their orientation, spacing, and height. Overly vegetative vines can also be slowed down by bending them.

At some point however, cutting part of the plant is usually required. This is actually a merciful action that serves several purposes for the vine. A loving, careful grower won't neglect it or allow the vine to grow wild, but instead intervene and gently but decisively redirect the plant's growth.

The French, who have devoted so much of their culture to wine, not surprisingly have a word for this – *élagage*. It sounds wonderfully elegant and refined, as if the plant should be delighted to receive this beneficent attention. We in the United States and England simply call it pruning. To our ears, it may sound harsh, punitive, and possibly demeaning. However, the French understand an aphorism shared by Jim Mitchell, a New England vintner who specializes in French-American grapes: *"to produce great wines, the vines must suffer, rather like athletes..."**

Sounds a bit like Paul (I Corinthians 9:24-27), doesn't it? From God's perspective, pruning is not sadistic or masochistic, but rather serves long-term goals. While most pruning does involve some suffering (or at least uninvited adjustments), not all suffering is pruning, and God can bring good out of any painful time. We should bear this in mind when we or others are going through difficult circumstances (Romans 8:28).

Due to differences in soil, terrain, rainfall, and climate, wine grape growers around the world vary their trellis patterns tremendously. German vineyards may have 3000 vines per acre; in parts of the United States, this number plummets below 400. Along the Rhine, one sees individual poles supporting sparse vines, in contrast with curtains of foliage found in California's Napa Valley. Just within France we encounter marvelous variation, from the short compact walls of vines in Bordeaux to umbrella-shaped bushes in the Rhône Valley. However, premium vineyards all share a common feature. They have thin, open canopies that achieve a precise "leaf arrangement."

Scientists have validated in recent decades what wine masters have known for centuries. A canopy needs to be about 1.4 leaves thick to maximally utilize the sun's light to transform water and carbon dioxide into sugars and acids required for the plant. More sun exposure is wasted on the leaf while more shade means less utility. Thus, the leaf arrangement is critical. Similarly, we are the leaves that God arranges – his workmanship for good purposes (read Eph 2:10, 4:11-13, I Cor 12, and Rom 12:4-5).

Each leaf can only use about 40% of the energy available on a sunny day, so having other leaves around helps. The best leaf arrangement allows for the tips to angle downward so that after being saturated they can reflect light onto lower levels. The plant as a whole does best when the individual leaves get ample exposure to the sun and share the surplus with their neighbors.

* Cox, Jeff, *From Vines to Wines*, 5th edition, Storey Publishing, North Adams, MA, 2015

Moreover, each community needs some diversity both in talents and seasons of life to thrive, and we all need to spend time with the Lord individually (Lk 10:38-42). Just as vines must slow down and stop producing new leaves in the summer to ripen grapes, we each must spend time with God to recharge before we can serve others. Maturity *and* youthful energy are both important. Older leaves provide relatively more nourishment for the plant but longevity depends on the newer leaves thriving. The wise pruner preserves the right mix. Vine growers often refer to balanced vines – balanced lives and communities are just as important.

You might ask, "if the goal is to capture all available sunlight, why not add a third layer of leaf depth in the canopy to use any light that breaks through?" One reason is too much shade hurts wine quality. Even more importantly, in the dark interior of a thick canopy, leaves don't photosynthesize enough to meet their own needs, let alone export nutrients. Every fall, deciduous plants shed their leaves precisely because with the diminishing daylight they're no longer productive enough to maintain their own needs and "autoprune." For the Christian life, participation is equally important – to grow and benefit others, we must faithfully respond to the truth and grace each of us is given.

Ultimately, pruning has several objectives. They are, according to one expert, "(a) to facilitate cultivation and gathering, (b) to increase the average yield, and (c) to improve the quality of fruit. Vines untouched by the pruner's knife bear irregularly; a year of over-bearing being followed by several of under-bearing as a consequence of exhaustion caused by a too severe drain on the reserve forces of the plant."* Another expert echoes -- "failure to reckon with this fact and maintain a proper mean between the two leads, on one hand, to comparative sterility, and on the other, to overbearing and premature exhaustion."** By periodically trimming back, the master gets not only better quality, but more sustainable – ultimately more productive – and more accessible (to the master and others) grapes.

Experienced vineyard managers also know that overpruning can leave too few grapes, and that cutting at the wrong place risks infection and death for the plant. They are sensitive to and avoid anything that would harm the vine in the long run. We can take comfort in knowing that our loving and sovereign

---

* Bioletti, FT, *Vine Pruning*. Read Books Ltd., Worcestershire, UK, 2013 (originally published by the University of California, 1897)
** Baldy, MW, *The University Wine Course: A Wine Appreciation Text & Self Tutorial*, Wine Appreciation Guild, San Francisco, CA, 2010

heavenly gardener understands our needs and his unique plans for us, even when our lives seem bent or even pruned. Thank God for his loving care and sustaining grace which enables us to rejoice in all things (Philippians 4:4)!

Thoughts for sharing:

1. Who gets pruned? Why? Is there a way to avoid being pruned?

2. How does God prune those who bear fruit?

3. Jesus frequently withdrew to lonely places to pray. Do you think he ever felt the risk of "overbearing and exhaustion"?

4. Have you ever felt overcommitted or distracted from deeper interests? Has your life ever been redirected in a way that was initially upsetting but in retrospect made you healthier, more productive, and/or more content? Read Luke 10:41-42, Matthew 11:28, and Mark 6:31. Do you think pruning can help save us from ourselves when we get too busy? How?

5. How do you know the difference between pruning and apparently unanswered prayer? Is knowing the difference important? Have you ever experienced an answer to prayer that was better than what you requested? Consider reading Philip Yancey's books *Disappointment with God* and *Prayer: Does It Make Any Difference?* to further explore these ideas.

6. Underpruning can potentially yield a large crop of sweet but unbalanced, poor quality wine grapes. Jesus

said we are to bear much fruit – should our focus be on quality or quantity? Why? What do you learn from Jesus' life?

7. Read James 1:2-6. The passage deals with "trials," but not explicitly pruning. How are the two different? How are they similar? What should our approach be to each?

8. Healthy vines have a good balance of mature and younger leaves. Do you know any members in your church outside your generation? How can you pray for them? How do you think their generation uniquely benefits the body of Christ? How can yours?

9. How can you better "spill light" onto others (p. 24, paragraph 2)? What do you first have to do?

– 6 –
HARVEST

Matthew 20 : 1 - 16

*For the kingdom of heaven is like a landowner who went
out early in the morning to hire laborers for his vineyard.
When he had agreed with the laborers for a denarius for the
day, he sent them into his vineyard. And he went out about
the third hour and saw others standing idle in the market
place; and to those he said, 'You also go into the vineyard,
and whatever is right I will give you.' And so they
went. Again he went out about the sixth and the ninth hour,
and did the same thing. And about the eleventh hour he
went out and found others standing around; and he said to
them,'Why have you been standing here idle all day
long?' They said to him,'Because no one hired us.' He said to
them, 'You go into the vineyard too.'*

"When evening came, the owner of the vineyard said to his foreman, 'Call the laborers and pay them their wages, beginning with the last group to the first.' When those hired about the eleventh hour came, each one received a denarius. When those hired first came, they thought that they would receive more; but each of them also received a denarius. When they received it, they grumbled at the landowner, saying, 'These last men have worked only one hour, and you have made them equal to us who have borne the burden and the scorching heat of the day.' But he answered and said to one of them, 'Friend, I am doing you no wrong; did you not agree with me for a denarius? Take what is yours and go, but I wish to give to this last man the same as to you. Is it not lawful for me to do what I wish with what is my own? Or is your eye envious because I am generous?' So the last shall be first, and the first last."

§

Agriculturally-rich France has several words for harvest. Given their love affair with wine, it's not surprising the French reserve one term for the celebrated gathering of wine grapes: *vendanger*. One may use *recolter* for olives or *moissoner* for wheat, but *la vendange* exclusively means the harvest of the precious fruit of the vine.

One of the greatest skills in winemaking is deciding exactly when *la vendange* should begin. The fruit gradually matures over months under the discerning eye of the vineyard manager. Masters aim for the exact peak of balance of acid and sugars to create the wine that he or she has in mind. They look for signs of *veraison*, when grapes accelerate toward maturity. Light green skin that earlier camouflaged them is recklessly abandoned for deeper colors. The grapes themselves seem to know they are ready to yield to their God-intended purpose. Many factors enter in to the human decision – the varietal, the style of wine, even what the weather is likely to do the next day.

Around September every year, the national consciousness of France begins to converge. Anticipation builds as the grapes fill out. When the time is right, the call goes out for helpers to harvest the focus of so much devotion, care, and concern. Although mechanical pickers have invaded some regions, in Champagne and others, thousands of workers still flood communities with a singular passion to collect the fruit for an ancient ritual: transforming it to wine.

Each community celebrates unique traditions echoing timeless dependence on the seasons of life. Even in long-urbanized Paris, several neighborhoods commemorate the event; some perpetuate centuries-old Roman habits whereas others are relatively recent rituals. What they all have in common is not a debate on the pickers' pay, but evenings spent sharing stories, singing, and laughing together. In many cases, the harvesters are treated to intimate private parties to appreciate hearty food and previous years' wine and the satisfaction of well-deserved rest from a long day in the vineyard.

It's probably not an accident that Matthew is the only one of the four evangelists who shares the parable of the vineyard workers. Themes from his own life are woven into its fabric. For example, three of the gospels record Matthew's calling by the Lord, yet his account is distinctive. Luke records that Jesus "noticed a tax-gatherer named Levi…" Matthew instead writes that Jesus "saw a man called Matthew, sitting in the tax office." Luke and Mark use the Hebrew *Levi*, *Matthew* chooses his Greek name that means "gift of God."

He distances himself from his prior occupation, downplaying Levi the tax collector who took from other Jews, favoring Matthew, the man who happened to be sitting in the tax office. All accounts agree however that once called, he immediately accepted Christ's invitation and soon hosted a great banquet out of gratitude. Levi's position had been lucrative, but Matthew unhesitatingly left it for an uncertain future with the Lord of life, grateful for the gift of a second chance and a different kind of reward.

Matthew pens more than half of all the New Testament instances of the word "reward" (*misthos*). Like grapes, Matthew clusters *"misthos"* nine times between 5:12 and 6:18, only using it in three other places. The first immediately follows the nine "blesseds" of the beatitudes. *Misthos* may be translated as good *or* bad consequences that naturally flow from an action, shorthand for the law of sowing and reaping.

With the Sermon on the Mount, Christ turns our understanding of blessedness and reward on its head, extending our view to the eternal. We learn the highest paid will be the Kingdom-possessors, the comforted, the earth-inheritors, the righteousness-satisfied, the mercy-granted, the God-seers, and finally the very children of God. To primarily seek other rewards is not to want more but to settle for less.

The remaining times Jesus discusses rewards in Matthew he refers to loving our enemies. He compels us to give to the needy, pray, and fast, all in secret, out of the limelight, secure of our eternal investment. He stresses the certainty of reward for the righteous, the merciful love-in-action friends: "whoever gives one of these little even a cup of cold water." Matthew's last *misthos* previews the Lord himself returning to reward according to what each has done. Not thought of, imagined, or dreamed, but done. Although we're saved by grace, we only fully experience the blessings of God's life when we participate and give of ourselves. Even more sobering, apparently most if not all of what God wants done in the world he depends on us humans to do, and our failure to obey results in pain, suffering, and loss for others as well.

Matthew alone also records the parable of the talents. When the master returns, he exclaims "well done, good and faithful servant" to those who invested proportionate to their gifts. They're granted full access to their master's joy. Tragically, the third servant acts out of fear and hid his talent in the earth, safe from harm but also from growth. He misses the risk, but also the joy.

God gives us talents not to safely guard, but to creatively, mysteriously partner with us to contribute to the goodness of the universe. Matthew 5:45 states, "he maketh his sun to rise on the just and the unjust..." God desires that all enjoy enduring benefit of his Kingdom, but won't force us to invest our gifts.

We often recoil at divine commands, suspecting privation. But the same God who told Moses (Deuteronomy 30:19) "choose life" came to live among us and commanded us to love so that we could share his deepest joy. Only from Matthew – the tax collector who became a gift from God – do we hear Jesus tell us what is appropriate to seek first (Matthew 6:33). The Lord does so because it doesn't come naturally for us. With gentlemanly deference to our will, he insists we find nothing short of eternal satisfaction. The grace is his, but the choice is ours. Our master rejoices when we demand for ourselves nothing less than the best wages.

Thoughts for sharing:

1. Why does God "hire" us? He could do things more efficiently in some other manner. Is it to achieve goals or produce fruit for God? Is it to experience his love and joy? Both? Is it possible for us to do either on our own?

2. Read Mt 19:16-26. What "good thing" can one do to acquire eternal life? What can we do to earn God's favor, make him love us more, or want to bless us more? Nothing! How does knowing that it is impossible for us to earn eternal life make you feel? What happens when people attempt the impossible?

3. What does God require of us? Is it possible for us to achieve it on our own? Read each of the scriptures below, then answer the question at the end:

Micah 6:8

> *He has told you, O man, what is good;*
> *And what does the LORD require of you*
> *But to do justice, to love kindness,*
> *And to walk humbly with your God?*

Matthew 23:23

> *Woe to you, scribes and Pharisees, hypocrites! For you tithe mint and dill and cummin, and have neglected the weightier provisions of the law: justice and mercy and faithfulness; but these are the things you should have done without neglecting the others.*

Matthew 22:36-40

> *"Teacher, which is the great commandment in the Law?" And He said to him, "'YOU SHALL LOVE THE LORD YOUR GOD WITH ALL YOUR HEART, AND WITH ALL YOUR SOUL, AND WITH ALL YOUR MIND.' This is the great and foremost commandment. The second is like it, 'YOU SHALL LOVE YOUR NEIGHBOR AS YOURSELF.' On these two commandments depend the whole Law and the Prophets."*

John 13:34

> *"A new commandment I give to you, that you love one another, even as I have loved you, that you also love one another. By this all men will know that you are My disciples, if you have love for one another."*

Question: What do these verses have in common?

Answer: God knows it's impossible for us to fulfill them on our own. Knowing he loves us anyway generates a gratitude that, when coupled with his grace, enables us to begin to live out his intentions.

4. Read the parable of the talents (Matthew 25:14-30):
   a. What do you think the man would have said if the servant had invested aggressively, but lost?
   b. Is that possible with the talents God gives us? What do you have to lose?
   c. Think about one worthwhile thing you would

attempt if you knew you couldn't lose. Do you think that may be a talent with which God's entrusted you? What keeps you from trying today?

5. CS Lewis wrote, "it would seem that our Lord finds our desires not too strong, but too weak. We are half-hearted creatures, fooling about with drink and sex and ambition when infinite joy is offered us, like an ignorant child who wants to go on making mud pies in a slum because he cannot imagine what is meant by the offer of a holiday at the sea. We are far too easily pleased." (*The Weight of Glory, and Other Addresses*) Are there any areas in your life that currently frustrate or tempt you that, when compared against the eternal goodness promised by God, seem to lose their power?

6. Ultimately, whether we admit it or not, we all want to be happy. In *Confessions*, Saint Augustine wrote he was moved to pursue Christianity after reading Cicero's *Hortensius*: "I was stirred to an earnest love of wisdom; and still I was deferring to reject mere earthly felicity..." He was looking for happiness and found something more profound – joy – in following Christ. Joy is the first fruit of the Spirit after love (Galatians 5:22-23), the express intent behind Christ's commandment to love each other (John 15:11), and the ultimate reward of the "good and faithful servants" (Matthew 25:23). Do you think most Christians seriously consider God's intense

desire for us to experience his joy, or do we, perhaps unconsciously, fear it's too good (too free, too wholesome, too *enjoyable*, etc.) to be true? Why?

7. The Westminster catechism claims "the chief end of man is to glorify God and enjoy him forever." Teddy Roosevelt claimed "Far and away the best prize that life has to offer is the chance to work hard at work worth doing." Are these assertions contradictory or complementary? Why?

FILLING

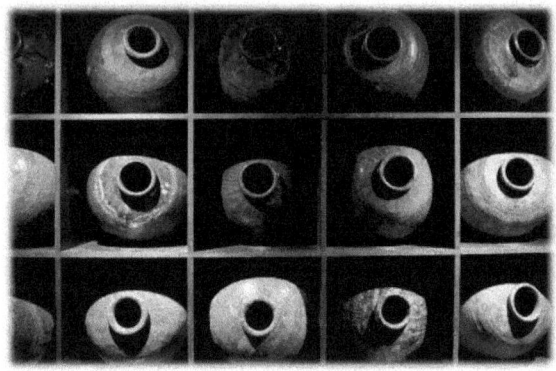

Luke 5:37-39

And no one puts new wine into old wineskins. If he does, the new wine will burst the skins and it will be spilled, and the skins will be destroyed. But new wine must be put into fresh wineskins. And no one after drinking old wine desires the new, for he says "the old is good."

§

Read Luke 5. Jesus evidently didn't have an MBA. He appears not to have been mentored in how to vet job applicants. Here he was, seeking to launch a global revolution, and he's content to stay in the lesser towns of a backwater Roman province. Worse, he has no apparent search criteria. His hiring campaign begins with three failed fishermen who've given up on their luck.

He then takes a break from recruiting to miraculously heal some outcasts, but fails to capitalize on the popularity, preferring instead to withdraw to lonely places and pray. He simply notices his next candidate before approaching to make his two-word pitch. The man is a tax collector named Levi who lines his pockets with surplus takings skimmed off the occupying government's taxes. Likely unscrupulous, definitely unpopular. Charles Carnegie would run the other way. Jesus trusted him to follow God and change the world. No resumé, no interview. Just a willingness to "follow me."

Without a question or hesitation, Levi leaves everything and celebrates with an elaborate party. All the tax collectors are there, considered by the Jews to be parasites if not outright traitors. The Pharisees gather around. Certainly Jesus would use the evening to preach to the congregated sinners. Instead, he *enjoys* himself, reclining at the table, eating and drinking with them all. So much so, indignant Pharisees pull his disciples aside side and ask "what's going on? How could a rabbi simply hang out with such people? No sermon. It almost appears as if he loves being with them."

Jesus hears the comments and calls out what would be obvious to those who care more for others than for one's prestige: he's around for those who see their need for Him.

Unsatisfied, the Pharisees turn to attack his disciples – apparently random, non-devout fishermen and now an impious tax collector. Disciples, everyone knows, are supposed to be devoted to God. They're special because they do special things that show it, like fasting and offering prayers. "We see our own disciples do such things, and John the Baptist's too," they proclaim. "But what's special about yours, Jesus? They still eat and drink like regular folk."

Jesus stops and perhaps pauses for dramatic effect before responding. Although the Pharisees didn't realize it, their questions reveal a fundamental misunderstanding of both the purpose of their life's activities and those of Jesus. Not only were they blind to their own shortcomings and deepest needs, they couldn't appreciate that the one who could satisfy them was standing in their presence.

God incarnate corrects their ignorance: religious rites fill in to bridge relationships, not the other way around. He also drops a bombshell. One fasts and prays to pierce through earthly veils and access God which isn't needed when He is at a party with you.

The Pharisees failed to see that what made Christ's disciples special wasn't what they did but whom they were with. They had left everything to be with him and would be rewarded with the vibrant, if not always predictable, life with the Creator of all things. In contrast, the Pharisees so sadly focused on satisfying laws they missed the Lawgiver, the Love-giver, in their midst.

Before the Pharisees have the chance to raise another objection, Jesus further turns the table with a double parable to point out why he chose his followers and not them. The disciples didn't assume they had it all figured out. They couldn't debate the nuances of arcane theological matters, but their souls profoundly appreciated the authority of Jesus and their need for him. They came first for the relationship, vulnerable and hungry. Out of humility, they allowed themselves time to understand as the Lord revealed truth through their shared life together.

The gospel writers themselves admitted they were frequently slow, but like new wineskins, their souls gradually filled in response to Christ's words and the grace of the Spirit as they obeyed the Lord.

Many well-respected authorities assert that Christ's teaching on the wineskin serves to distinguish between law and grace, the Old Testament and the New

Covenant. But likely the real issue here is the human heart. Both Matthew's and Mark's accounts end harshly with the destruction of the old wineskin by new wine. Luke however sensitively portrays the humanity of both Jesus and the Pharisees.

Jesus acknowledges the all-too-human tendency to cling to what is known and to what can be controlled: "the old is better." He laments inability to penetrate a heart that's stiff. For his teachings to take hold, for his followers to experience the joy he desires for them, they must be open and supple enough to humbly stretch their concept of what it means to live with God.

It's the same with us today. We're not special because of how much we give, our eduction or skills, the oratory of our prayers, or the positions we happen to have. We're special because the one who created us says so. He came among us. He gave his life so we could know him. When we abide in him – whether in a party or a prayer closet – we connect the source of truth. When his life flows through us, we find his joy.

The words disciple and discipline connote a degree of ascetic sternness, but they both derive from the Latin word *discere* which simply means to learn. The Christian life is about learning to follow and yield to God's spirit more than executing rigorous self-imposed restrictions. Learning, as at school, requires time patiently spent with the teacher listening, answering, and practicing. The question for us is, "are we content to know about him or do we really want to know him?" If the latter, prepare to be stretched.

    The third Thursday of November each year, wine sellers from southern Burgundy release weeks-old *Beaujolais nouveau* to eager buyers around the world. By law, Gamay grapes are hand-picked in a hilly region only 8 miles wide just outside Lyon, then undergo a ununusal fermentation process* which uniquely transforms the grape whole and intact, yielding a fruit-rich product with very little bitterness. In contrast with virtually all other wines that are intentionally aged to improve flavor, this one is as much a celebration of the recent harvest – and the community and culture it represents – as its flavor.
.

    Unlike the superficial, rigid observation of traditional rites, Christ's dynamic love can also transform our whole being and our unique needs, talents, and personality into something quite special that distinctly blesses others: full in fruit, low in bitterness. His means will seldom be

---

* carbonic maceration

what we expect, but following him keeps us fresh and relevant to other's lives.   God's new wine is good that way.

Thoughts for sharing:

1. What personal ideas or practices have changed the most compared to when you weren't a Christian? In what ways have your beliefs and/or behaviors changed as you've matured in faith?

2. Seeing things in a new light can be healthy, even when it challenges us. At times, changing a ritual exposes the heart of the issue behind the practice. When you visit another congregation or hear a different point of view, do we reflexively mutter "the old is good" before testing to see if it really is (I Thessalonians 5:21)?

Tradition is not necessarily bad, and often contributes powerfully to comfort, significance, and stability in communities. Under what circumstances would you be willing to let go or change your traditions, attitudes, or assumptions?

It has been said that clinging to the past won't bring it back, but can prevent us from embracing the future in times of change. Are there any traditions in your church, work, or family that you should let go of? Anything new to embrace? What would you refuse to let go of? How do you determine?

3. How do we keep ourselves open and fresh? Read 2 Peter 1:3-8.

4. Paul strove to be "all things to all men" (I Corinthians 9:19-23) and at times limited his own freedom in grace so as to not make others stumble. What are possible areas in which you feel you have freedom but in certain contexts may be spiritually appropriate to limit so as to not cause difficulties for others? What factors should be considered? (Yes, wine consumption could potentially fall in this category! There are many of sincere Christians who drink as well as those who don't.) Conversely, what if you feel others are being taking advantage of grace to pursue wrong behavior? As time permits, read Colossians 2 and discuss.

5. Jesus and his disciples were welcome guests at Levi's feast where "tax collectors and sinners" didn't feel threatened, but likely enjoyed the evening. How do we lovingly remain relevant and winsome to those outside the Christian faith while maintaining our integrity?

6. Although Jesus downplays his own disciples' need for externally obvious fasting and prayer, he doesn't dismiss the need for both. In fact, in Mt 17:21 we read that some challenges required both for his followers. How do you approach prayer in your life? Mt 6:16-18 implies that Jesus expects his contemporaries fasted. In the Old Testament, fasting was only "officially" prescribed for the Day of the Atonement. Consider discussing

Leviticus 16:29-30, 23:27-32, 2 Samuel 12:15-17, Psalm 35:13-14, Isaiah 58:3-12, Matthew 6:16-18, and Acts 27:9. What is your perspective on fasting in modern world? Are there other things than food that we could consider giving up periodically for spiritual benefit?

7. The Babylonian Talmud records a story of an emperor's daughter who disliked the common clay jars used to hold their family wine. "You should keep our wine in jars of gold and silver!" she protested to her father.* He complied and the drink quickly turned sour. Rabbis use this tale to explain how often the humble things in our lives are needed to convey the most important truths.

    All of us can find areas in our lives in which at least one other person appears to be more gifted. Have you ever considered that your relative lack in this area may be just as important, even necessary to God? Paul himself said he rejoiced in his weakness. How can you glorify God with your strengths AND your weaknesses?

---

* *Talmud Bavli Nedarim 50b*

TRANSMISSION

Luke 22:14-20

When the hour had come, He reclined at the table, and the apostles with Him. And He said to them, "I have earnestly desired to eat this Passover with you before I suffer; for I say to you, I shall never again eat it until it is fulfilled in the kingdom of God." And when He had taken a cup and given thanks, He said, "Take this and share it among yourselves; for I say to you, I will not drink of the fruit of the vine from now on until the kingdom of God comes." And when He had taken some bread and given thanks, He broke it and gave it to them, saying, "This is My body which is given for you; do this in remembrance of Me." And in the same way He took the cup after they had eaten, saying, "This cup which is poured out for you is the new covenant in My blood."

§

They gathered around the table upstairs, the same twelve men who marveled three years before when the one in the middle turned water to wine. Life had seemed to be just starting. Now it was late, they were tired, and everything was falling apart. The one who had changed their lives, who had given them hope, for whom they had given up everything, seemed to be passively, perhaps helplessly, allowing momentum to fade into obscurity and mortal risk. The meal that for millennia commemorated God's special protection would now be their last together, a somber reminder of what could have been. A bittersweet tribute to a man who had done amazing things and lifted their horizons perhaps, but in the end, just like everything else in life, been overcome by circumstances.

They didn't know it yet, but as in Cana there were again witnessing a beginning. But all they could hear is he would be leaving them with only the hollow hope of a memorial rite. His language was beyond distinctive; it was disturbing. The one they had seen for years gently welcome children and tenderly heal the sick now spoke of drinking his blood. The rabbi that had quoted the law and prophets now, on the eve of his departure, implied a new, different way. Had he in the end given up, readjusted his expectations? Was this the stiff upper lip of a resolute rabbi trying to keep their despair at bay?

What possible good could this wine do for them at this dark hour and in the days to come? That none of them cried out in protest or disbelief is remarkable.

For over 2,000 years it is has remained an unabashed mystery of the Christian faith just what is represented in communion. Even Paul admits a only dim view of what the Redeemer of the cosmos achieved, what ethereal force was transmitted to us mere mortals while the God-man was beaten, cursed, nailed and hung to expire in ignominy. What the Creator did to fix the universe and us, His broken body.

The physics of the world he created offers us clues. 92,960,000 miles away, our sun continuously sends unfathomable energy as photons, packets of energy that inexplicably travel simultaneously as massless particles *and* waves. Less than 0.000000045292% of the sun's energy reaches our earth's surface, yet this paltry sum is terrifying enough to make the oceans churn, hurricanes howl, and thunder peal. Enough to give voice to every lion's roar, lift every eagle's flight, propel every whale's dive, and contract every single beat of every single human heart. All life that has ever existed here has been sustained by just a billionth of the power of just one very average star out of more than an estimated 50,000,000,000,000,000,000,000 in the observable universe. Our loudest shouts, our most violent protests, our most strident demands aren't even cosmic whispers.

Still, the tender cry of a hurting heart was enough to bring God himself into our world, willing to be swallowed up in the pain and seeming insignificance of our existence.

Life on this planet begins when a photon, one of those ubiquitous but incomprehensible wave-particle dualities from the heavens pierces the veil of our atmosphere and without our notice is swallowed into a humble paper-thin leaf. Thousands of years from the core to the surface of the sun, then 8 minutes across 92 million miles, less than a second on earth, then gone. Millions of times every second of every day.

The magic inside the leaft starts when a photon strikes chlorophyll, a unique molecule belonging to a larger class of structures called porphyrin rings. In chlorophyll, the porphyrin ring contains a single magnesium atom at the center. The photon transfers the sun's energy to the ring, propelling an electron along a path that ultimately creates sugar, the fundamental food for earth's life. If the leaf happens to be on a grape vine, its sugars are transported to grapes and stored until they are ready to be broken down into alcohol, carbon dioxide, and water by yeast to make wine. Oxygen, by the way, is produced as a byproduct.

Humans have porphyrin rings as well, but with an iron atom in the middle instead of magnesium. A seemingly small difference, but it's essentially what separates chlorophyll from blood. The first gives plants life and creates oxygen. The second* sustains our life with that oxygen. In an even more amazing and elegant mystery, Christ's life, death, and resurrection on earth enabled the transfer of His divine energy, His Spirit, to sustain us eternally.

   A separate class of plant molecules affords us a different view into God's life. Polyphenols are common compounds that plants have developed as a natural sunscreen and antioxidant. The most visually striking ones are anthocyanins, purple and red pigments that spellbind New England foliage-watchers every fall and imbue Cabernet Sauvingon grapes with their deep garnet hue. The most widespread polyphenols are tannins, found in fruit skins and bark around the world. Tannins contribute dry, bitter complexity to black tea, dark chocolate, and red wine. They're also the elements that enable the best reds to improve with time.

The molecule is called heme, four of which make hemoglobin.

Many studies suggest the benefits that plants receive from the polyphenol antioxidants they generate are transferrable to consumers. If true, in drinking wine we internalize protection achieved by another's efforts. Christ, in an even more mysterious fashion, transfers his life to us through grace achieved by his being crushed. The concept isn't alien to other religions. Some Hindus and others hint at what Mahayana Buddhists teach as "merit transfer." Something profound and irrepressible in the human spirit seems to know our inadequacies can only satisfied by another and yearns to know Him.

His truth contains elements of each of these analogies. The sun's energy would vaporize plants anywhere near the source, yet God's pathways harness it to create all the beauty of a delicate rose. The infinite power that would kill man if seen directly (Exodus 33:20), humbled Himself and died to give us life instead. We are sustained by that divine energy. As we remain in him and consume the wine of his covenant, we take in grace against death, and can even appreciate bitterness that, in divinely crafted vessels, can be transformed into complex richness over time.

From the production of grapes to their transformation into wine, the process hinges on the sun's energy coming into our world as a mysterious-yet-common dual wave-particle then disappearing in a "simple," fragile, likely unseen leaf.

Now for the rest of the story: what becomes of the photon? Although it's still a mystery, the word physicists most often use is "consumed." Consumed, as in "I in you." The massless particle, the essential paradox of the physics of our universe that transmits energy from the heavens to us, the dual-natured Energy-bearer, can only transmit life by being consumed and abiding within.

As mysterious as photons, photosynthesis and the new covenant remain, they're the necessary and fundamental stuff of reality. Even without understanding the physics that makes oxygen and carries it through blood, every breath we take sustains our flesh. Even without comprehending the metaphysical change that God's blood achieved for us on the cross, we can be confident it sustains our souls. Each time we celebrate the Passover in the Kingdom, may we know and drink deeply of his love and share it richly with others to know the joy he intends. We're blessed to know today looking forward what the disciples had to learn looking back. Their last meal celebrated the beginning of all that is best.

Thoughts for sharing:

1. What is the new covenant Jesus refers to? What was the previous one? Did God change his mind or was this his intention all along?

2. Has the kingdom of God come already? When? What has been fulfilled in it?

3. The disciples were to share the cup among themselves. Are we called to share anything among ourselves in the Church? Can we truly enjoy and multiply the joys in each other's lives without sharing some of the challenges?

4. What do you think it means that his body was "given for you"? Are we expected to give anything in response?

5. In what ways are we to imitate Christ? What should be our motivation? Are there ways in which we shouldn't or can't?

6. Is it a Christian responsibility to help protect others in difficulties? What are some ways we do that?

7. 2 Corinthians 1:3-5 reads, *"praise be to the God and Father of our Lord Jesus Christ, the Father of compassion and the God of all comfort, who comforts us in all our troubles, so that we can comfort those in any trouble with the comfort we ourselves receive from God. For just as we share abundantly*

in the sufferings of Christ, so also our comfort abounds through Christ." What experiences in your life have helped you help others? Were all of them pleasant, or have some been difficult?

8. Galatians 6:2 says, *"carry each other's burdens, and in this way you will fulfill the law of Christ."* What do you think is the law of Christ? How do you view the role of serving others in the Christian life?

– 9 –
TRANSFORMATION

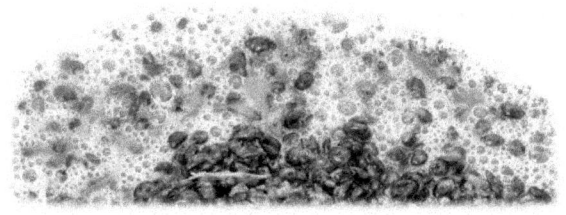

John 19:28-30

... knowing that everything had now been finished, and so that Scripture would be fulfilled, Jesus said, "I am thirsty." A jar of wine vinegar was there, so they soaked a sponge in it, put the sponge on a stalk of the hyssop plant, and lifted it to Jesus' lips. When he had received the drink, Jesus said, "It is finished." With that, he bowed his head and gave up his spirit.

§

In the previous chapter, we explored the flow of life's energy from the sun to plants to us. Genesis and scientists agree that plants came before the animals, creating the oxygen that would sustain the latter. All non-plant life from bacteria to humans use similar pathways to initially break down sugar for energy. Higher organisms like us then extract even more energy through advanced metabolic pathways.

But what if there's no oxygen? What if we become bankrupt in our most important resource? When we come up short, there is another pathway available. If our bodies work harder and faster than oxygen can be supplied, we briefly shift gears to a less efficient process that creates lactic acid as a byproduct. We feel the acid burning in our muscles during a strenuous workout – we make do, but it's not comfortable.

Some primitive organisms like yeast also have this capacity to "breathe" without oxygen, but as their *primary* means of energy conversion. This is fermentation, derived from a Latin word meaning anger or passion, presumably because of the roiling activity observed in a fermenting vessel. In the process yeasts create carbon dioxide (think leavened bread) like humans. They also create something totally alien to human metabolism: alcohol. Every time we drink wine, we confess our dependence on another life's achievement. We acknowledge our futility and the grace of otherness.

These abilities have been harnessed and celebrated for millennia. However, the science behind fermentations has only recently been discovered. Before Louis Pasteur, it was poorly understood and at times even dangerous.

The first sparking wines of Champagne were the unintended result of northern France's chilly climate. To the dismay of vintners, their product unpredictably exploded bottles. We now know the region's cool temperatures prematurely and temporarily stopped fermentation in autumn. With spring warmth, more pressure-generating carbon dioxide was again generated. Ironically, Dom Perignon, the monk commonly associated with Champagne, tried to *prevent* the bubbly carbonation in his cellars. It was across the Channel where sturdier industrial glassmaking techniques allowed the British to first deliberately create and popularize sparkling wine, now a mainstay of the *champenoise* economy.

Two centuries after the English perfected the pop in Champagne, Pasteur linked yeast with this potent process. Although he identified the organism, he admitted *"if asked, in what consists the chemical act whereby the sugar is decomposed . . . I am completely ignorant of it."* He knew there was a living source, but not the means.

Similarly, Jesus told the Nicodemus in John 3:8, *"The wind blows where it wishes and you hear the sound of it, but do not see where it comes from and where it is going; so it is with everyone born of the Spirit."* Something in our souls appreciates the unpredictable freedom of life, even though it may create anxiety at times.

But what happens when life is *too* wild, out of control? The same one who fashioned us from stardust on a thin wafer of habitable area less than 0.1% of the volume of our planet. The earth's grandeur virtually vanishes against the backdrop of a universe of life-crushing extremes, governed by laws that simultaneously, wondrously permit and fine-tune our hospitable home.

Our God fashioned an island of vitality from an ocean of unfathomably harsh forces. A creator like that isn't surprised or panicked when we learn after much pain that we can't fix ourselves. From the foundation of the world, he provided a solution to do what humans need but can't for themselves: sustainably breathe life from another source, drink wine created by a new means.

Shortly after celebrating the last supper with a cup and loaf of bread, Christ the man knelt and pleaded for the cup to be taken away if possible. He then lovingly, fatally embraced the eternal plan that permeated his divine nature, and set his face for Golgotha. The wine of life contaminated by human spoilage could only be drunk by him.

Toward the end of his six agonizing hours hanging on the cross, all the gospels share several similar details. We read Christ accepted a drink of vinegar, satisfying prophecy from the 69th psalm. Vinegar (from Latin for "sour wine") results when bacteria ferment the wine, producing acid instead of alcohol, a reminder to us what a difference the leaven makes in wine as well as the spiritual life (See Luke 12:1, Matthew 16:6, Mark 8:13-1.)

Following that, he cried out "it is finished!" Christ took the vinegar as the last of innumerable Old Testament prophecies he satisfied from Genesis to Malachi. He then resolutely gave up his spirit, commenting beforehand: "No man takes it from me, I lay it down of my own accord" (John 10:18). He finished with courage, resolve and love, all the things we call most noble.

From beginning to end, God had come to give abundant life (John 10:10). Unlike the leaven of the Pharisees, Sadducees and Herodians – our tendencies toward self-righteous hypocrisy, doubt, and political gain (Matthew 16:6, Mark 8:15, Luke 12:1) – his leaven makes life-sustaining bread that *increases* with consumption (Matthew 14:13-21).

While we were bankrupt and unable to find enduring life through our own means, the yeast of Christ's cup achieved it through His consumption and death. His plan called forth an older, deeper, more primal means that didn't rely on humans, latecomers to Creation's party.

Christ began his ministry selflessly creating wine for others to enjoy and finished by accepting Roman vinegar – our spoiled wine and lives – on the cross. Betrayed and forsaken by friends, he swallowed our mocking, ignorance, hatred, and violence. In the tomb, his fermentation – his *passion* – unhinged the decaying process of our futile, errant attempts at finding life.

The Lord and Master of all emerged three days later to celebrate the cosmic Passover as promised to his disciples. He did what we couldn't, the great reversal, transforming our bitter vinegar into the wine of the new covenant: unspoiled, unending, unlimited love. Amen, amen, and amen!

Thoughts for sharing:

1. Left alone, bacteria quickly spoil milk. However, if we add the enzyme rennet and control a few factors, the same process of fermentation can make cheese, wine's marriage partner. France alone has over 300 varieties!

How can God help you transform the sour milk in your life and relationships into something savory? Consider the following two verses:

> II Corinthians 1:3-7: *Praise be to the God and Father of our Lord Jesus Christ, the Father of compassion and the God of all comfort, who comforts us in all our troubles, so that we can comfort those in any trouble with the comfort we ourselves receive from God. For just as we share abundantly in the sufferings of Christ, so also our comfort abounds through Christ.*

> Colossians 3:12-14: *Therefore, as God's chosen people, holy and dearly loved, clothe yourselves with compassion, kindness, humility, gentleness and patience. Bear with each other and forgive one another if any of you has a grievance against someone. Forgive as the Lord forgave you. And over all these virtues put on love, which binds them all together in perfect unity.*

2. Producing the right wine or cheese requires we choose the right leaven and feed it the right energy source. How do we obtain peace, one of the fruits of the Spirit (Galatians 5:22-23)?

How do the below verses apply?

John 14:27: *"Peace I leave with you; my peace I give you. I do not give to you as the world gives. Do not let your hearts be troubled and do not be afraid."*

Philippians 4:6-8: *Do not be anxious about anything, but in every situation, by prayer and petition, with thanksgiving, present your requests to God. And the peace of God, which transcends all understanding, will guard your hearts and your minds in Christ Jesus.*
Finally, brothers and sisters, whatever is true, whatever is noble, whatever is right, whatever is pure, whatever is lovely, whatever is admirable—if anything is excellent or praiseworthy—think about such things. Whatever you have learned or received or heard from me, or seen in me—put it into practice. And the God of peace will be with you.

3. John F. Kennedy once said that the law of life is change. Our earthly lives don't stand still; they move in one direction. We're not asked to be born, and as we age we're not asked if we like the changes. We're only given the choice how to respond.

Fermentation breaks down complex molecules into simpler ones in a process some have called "controlled spoilage." We select microorganims to manipulate a process that would otherwise rush toward natural decay to achieve transformation and preservation instead. Read Jesus' attitude toward his life and "controlled decay" (John 10:17-18): *"For this reason the Father loves Me, because I lay down My life so that I may take it again. No one has taken it away from Me, but I lay it down on My own initiative. I have authority to lay it down, and I have authority to take it up again."* How does Jesus' confidence inspire, encourage, or influence you?

Jim Elliott, a missionary pilot who died serving in Ecuador, once said "He is no fool who gives what he cannot keep to gain what he cannot lose." What are some of the gifts, talents, or resources you think God is calling you to give away (or invest, depending on your perspective) to bless others?

4. At times we find ourselves in painful circumstances and uncertain how to react. We may be treated poorly by others acting out of ignorance or inspired by selfish, even hurtful motives. Is it possible to neutralize or even reverse the leaven in those situations? Consider Romans 12:9-21 below.

"Love must be sincere. Hate what is evil; cling to what is good. Be devoted to one another in love. Honor one another above yourselves. Never be lacking in zeal, but keep your spiritual fervor, serving the Lord. Be joyful in hope, patient in affliction, faithful in prayer. Share with the Lord's people who are in need. Practice hospitality.

Bless those who persecute you; bless and do not curse. Rejoice with those who rejoice; mourn with those who mourn. Live in harmony with one another. Do not be proud, but be willing to associate with people of low position. Do not be conceited.

> *Do not repay anyone evil for evil. Be careful to do what is right in the eyes of everyone. If it is possible, as far as it depends on you, live at peace with everyone. Do not take revenge, my dear friends, but leave room for God's wrath, for it is written: "It is mine to avenge; I will repay," says the Lord. On the contrary:*
>
> > *'If your enemy is hungry, feed him;*
> > *if he is thirsty, give him something to drink.*
> > *In doing this, you will heap burning coals*
> > *on his head.'*
>
> > *"Do not be overcome by evil,*
> > *but overcome evil with good."*

5.   In Matthew 5:13-16, Jesus says, *"You are the salt of the earth. But if the salt loses its saltiness, how can it be made salty again? It is no longer good for anything, except to be thrown out and trampled underfoot."*

The desirable bacteria that create cheese also preserve it by making the environment too acidic for other species to survive. Only by filling with the good is the bad kept out. Each of us is born with a soul needing to be filled; if the authentic best isn't found, we'll all too often cling to whatever apparent good our being strives to find around us.

God calls us to be salt, a flavoring agent and preservative. However, we can't be both by vacuum-sealing a sterile existence. Generally, Christian salt is least helpful condemning others' weaknesses and vices.

More often, we can be effective adopting salt's other virtue, a flavor enhancer that helps others appreciate of the truly good. Rather than attempting to remove the symptoms of thirst and hunger, we're to help them find the source of "living water and bread of life." That begins with our own lives. How do we demonstrate God's goodness and reality to the world around us?

– 10 –

POURING

Philippians 2:5-7, 17

Have this attitude in yourselves which was also in Christ Jesus, who, although He existed in the form of God, did not regard equality with God a thing to be grasped, but emptied Himself, taking the form of a bond-servant, and being made in the likeness of men. Being found in appearance as a man, He humbled Himself by becoming obedient to the point of death, even death on a cross... But even if I am being poured out as a drink offering upon the sacrifice and service of your faith, I rejoice and share my joy with you all. You too, I urge you, rejoice in the same way and share your joy with me.

§

We tend to label more precisely what we know well. We typically refine our vocabulary to better describe what we need to understand the most. Anthropologist Franz Boas claimed Canadian Inuits have over 50 different words for snow such as *aqilokoq* for "softly falling snow" and *piegnartoq* for "snow that is good for driving sleds"! As we've discovered, the French celebrate their admiration for wine through distinctive terms for harvesting. Unfortunately however, there is no special French word for pouring wine, the climactic scene in a multi-year series of performances. The host can thereafter do no more; the experience is now consummated and appreciated – or not – by the guest.

Fortunately for us, the apostle Paul expressed Christ's life with precision in passages like Philippians 2:5-7:

"In your relationships with one another, have the same mindset as Christ Jesus: Who, being in very nature God, did not consider equality with God something to be used to his own advantage; rather, he made himself nothing by taking the very nature of a servant, being made in human likeness."

Paul's phrase "made himself nothing" (or "of no reputation") emerges from the Greek verb *kenóō*, "to empty, make void, or neutralize." The same word is only used in four other places in the New Testament (Romans 4:14, I Corinthians 1:17, I Corinthians 9:15, 2 Corinthians 9:3), all by Paul for the same effect.

At the very end of a verse moments later (Phil 2:16), Paul uses a related term to emphasize his life's focus: *"And then I will be able to boast on the day of Christ that I did not run or labor in vain."* He continues, *"But even if I am being poured out like a drink offering on the sacrifice and service coming from your faith, I am glad and rejoice with all of you."*

Here Paul uses a rarer, even more precious verb – *spendō* – "to pour out." Like a costly drop of perfume, Paul sparingly reserves *spendō* for only one other passage as he resolutely eyes his own cross: *"For I am already being poured out like a drink offering, and the time for my departure is near. I have fought the good fight, I have finished the race, I have kept the faith."* (II Timothy 2:6-7)

In high school, I lived in Bolivia where many still observed an Incan custom of pouring of small amount of fermented beverage on the earth before drinking. The rite honored *Pachamama* – the Mother Earth goddess – and its effect visually registers as the drops hit the soil, absorbed back into the arid land from which it came. I still remember standing in a eucalyptus-redolent mining town high in the Andes during Easter week as villagers poured *chicha* on the ground then offered me some to drink, welcoming me into their their community.

Paul's readers would have had been familiar with the practice. Drink offerings were a part of Greek, Roman, and Jewish observances. In the first phase of Paul's career, he vigorously – even violently – established himself as a diligent defender of religious tradition. Encountering Christ however compelled him to count his hard-earned gains as loss, sacrificing security and respect for uncertainty and suffering.

In the confines of a Roman prison, he wrote to the church at Philippi during a period of tremendous personal difficulty. Yet the theme of his epistle is joy, pouring himself back to into the Source of his existence and blessing. For Paul, joy is so fundamental to life that while other New Testament writers use it – the ancient Greek word *chairō* – as a greeting, he alone adapts it for farewell (2 Corinthians 13:11).

If there is an ideal tongue for communicating the eternal multifaceted truths of God's actions between Good Friday and Easter Sunday in one word, it could very well be modern French. *Verser* is most frequently translated as "to pour." But many Parisians will tell you *verser* also commonly means to empty, bridging both Christ's (*kenóŏ*) and Paul's (*spendō*). Remarkably, *verser* can also mean to pay, cancel a debt or punishment, shed tears or blood, overturn, and/or wash. That single utterance virtually exhausts the theologian's lexicon for Christ's achievements on our behalf. In the Beginning, the word *verser* was almost certainly with God.

French Renaissance author Michel de Montaigne wrote, *"Versez leur du bon vin, ils vous feront de bonnes lois"* ("Pour them good wine and they will make you good laws"), revealing truth about human community and reciprocity. Even more profoundly, God has poured out himself as the good wine of the new covenant <u>*and*</u> demonstrated for us the very best law: the law of Christ, bearing each others' burdens (Galatians 6:2). We are to have the same attitude as Christ, pouring out ourselves for others. Only an empty vessel can be filled with something new, God's joy, in exchange.

According to John, Jesus started his ministry bringing joy to Cana (2:10) and ended commanding his disciples to empty themselves in each others' lives so their joy would be full (15:11-12). Paul also juxtaposed being poured out and encouraging others to share in blessed contentedness. God our creator consistently calls us in his image to participate in the highest creative privilege of generating joy and sharing with others. To drink and in turn *be* the good wine: chosen, transformed, and served in response to God-initiated love, the most powerful force of the cosmos. To pour out joy, the longing of every human heart.

Thoughts for sharing:

1. According to Paul in the passage above, what is our attitude to be?

2. In what ways did Christ not seek to attain equality with God? How did Jesus humble himself? How should this affect our self-image and pursuits?

   Many of us feel we need to achieve much in the eyes of others, whereas Christ, who could have had all the world, "made himself nothing (or without reknown)." What is the difference between good and great? (Go to www.merriam-webster.com if unsure.) Which one should we strive for? Consider that Christ never wrote one word for posterity, yet the Bible is the best-selling book of all time.

3. British literary and art critic GK Chesterton commented, "The Christian ideal has not been tried and found wanting; it has been found difficult and not tried." How do you think this applies to Christ's and Paul's teaching about joy?

4. CS Lewis wrote that throughout his life he was haunted by intermittent pangs of a unique aspect of joy – the German word is *Sehnsucht* – "an unsatisfied desire which is itself more desirable than any other satisfaction." According to one author, "for Lewis, joy is

at the heart of Christianity – it is the gigantic secret that compels women and men into the company of the Cross and characterizes the fruit of their sufferings... As Lewis grew in his faith, there would be no detour around the tears and tribulations of life – of being stomped, pressed down, and crushed like grapes – so that the sweet wine of intoxicating laughter could be poured out on dry, thirsty souls."

Lewis claimed "Our best havings are wantings," and the passion of *Sehnsucht* pointed him toward eternity, toward the unfulfilled yet hinted at joys of heaven. Do you agree with Lewis that joy is a key theme and goal, even a commandment – in Christianity? Why or why not? Considering the Sermon on the Mount, is that joy to be experienced here and now, or deferred until heaven?*

5. Mathieu Ricard, once dubbed the "world's happiest man" due to remarkably high level of gamma wave activity in his brain, published a book on the source of his emotional state – *Altruism* – in 2015. He told one journalist, "It's a natural effect: You are open and kind to others, and without even noticing, you are happy,"** Ricard cites data from brain imaging that demonstrates giving may actually be more biologically pleasurable than receiving, and continued practice can actually change the way the brain is wired.

How do such findings relate to New Testament verses on loving others and finding joy? Do you think our capacity to love and find joy is programmed in our biology by our Creator, is given to us by the Lord supernaturally, or both?

* All quotes from, Lindvall, T, "Joy and Sehnsucht: the laughter and longings of C.S. Lewis," *Mars Hill Review*, 1997; 8(Summer): 25-38
http://www.leaderu.com/marshill/mhr08/hall1.html)
** Gregoire, C:
http://www.huffingtonpost.com/2015/07/16/matthieu-ricard-altruism_n_7795988.html

EPILOGUE

Luke 22:27

For who is greater, the one who is at the table or the one who serves? Is it not the one who is at the table? But I am among you as one who serves.

§

I recently walked through the streets of a tropical riverside town in a former French colony during monsoon season. The nation's history is, like many, one of multiple waves of invasion, subjugation, and liberation with a newly assimilated identity. Despite the colonial period's dark side, elements of European culture have been preserved with a sense of residual prestige. That muggy afternoon, passing by knock-off clothing stores and fruit markets, I encountered several kiosks proudly displaying velveteen-wrapped bottles of wine that vendors hawked like t-shirts on the sidewalk.

Whatever worthwhile qualities those wines might have once possessed were damaged by the exposure to the intense heat and light. Unwitting or uncaring, the merchants had neglected the maintenance of a dynamic product. France had left decades previously, and although the some of the charm of its culture remained, without the passionate care and attention of knowledgeable merchants from product's place of origin, the alien alluring beverages degraded from marvellous to unpalatable. Doubtlessly, some hapless customer's first taste of wine came from one of those stands, leaving her wondering what the fuss was about.

The same thing can happen in the Christian life. The glory and enthusiasm of our early growth can, if left unattended, wither in the languid heat of life's circumstances. On our own, we're at risk of becoming insipid, unbalanced, and possibly bitter. Others may see us see us – the visible, tangible, audible body of Christ – while the custodian has been away, and wonder what the fuss was about.

How do we maintain the good? John 8:31-32 provides a virtuous cycle: faith from knowing God's word leads to abiding in prayer and practice which results in knowing divine truth in a deeper sense that inspires even greater faith. That's not to say storms won't blow. Sweltering heat and weltering storms will come to the faithful and unbeliever alike. Paul confessed (I Corinthians 15:19) that if Christian hope is rooted only in this world, then we of all people are to be most pitied. But the wise will listen to revealed truth and act in love to hold fast and emerge resilient, eyes focused on our eternal goals.

At the last supper, Jesus reminded his disciples of our tendency to vaunt ourselves over others, adding (Luke 22:26-27), "*...But you are not to be like that. Instead, the greatest among you should be like the youngest, and the one who rules like the one who serves.*" Christ knew we're primarily made for love, not promotion. Our fulfillment in the Kingdom comes as servants, not celebrities.

After counting the cost to purchase quality wine, proper care is still required. It will forever be your bottle, but how much you and others enjoy the contents depends on continued investment in maintenance. We are freely given access to God's kingdom vineyard, but reaping truth, grace, and joy is proportionate to how faithfully we "work out (our) salvation..." (Philippians 2:12) and live as he did (Luke 9:23, I John 2:6) in relationship with the master.

Galileo, marveling at the manifestations of the Creator's power, once said, "the sun, with all those planets revolving around it and dependent on it, can still ripen a bunch of grapes as if it had nothing else in the universe to do." God demonstrates infinite humility in allowing us to share in his creative joy and depending on us to pour out the fruit of His Spirit on the world He loves. Like Jesus at the Cana wedding, do we serve our very best? The universe celebrates with us when we do.

SUR LIE

The French phrase *sur lie* means 'on the lees,' the residual yeast left after fermentation. Some great wines (Chardonnay, Champagne, Muscadet) are not filtered, but intentionally left on the spent leaven to achieve effects like hazelnut flavor, increased complexity, mellowed oak, and enhanced freshness, color, and clarity.

The residual questions below may be used at the end of the book or to enrich the discussion after any lesson (parentheses provide suggested best chapter match). An American author once once quipped, "a bottle of wine begs to be shared; I have never met a miserly wine lover." God's truth and love are meant to be shared as well. As satisfying as lifting a glass in celebration may be, lifting each other up is God's joy-purposed command for us.

§

1. (Ch. 2) In John 21, Jesus commands Peter to follow and feed his sheep. Peter perhaps intuited it could mean his death. He sees John nearby and asks: "Lord, and what about this man?" Jesus replies, "If I want him to remain until I come, what is that to you? You follow Me!" Each of us has a unique DNA, background, gifts and shortcomings. Each of us is also called to a unique journey with Christ.

Our faithfulness yields a beautiful, unique aroma (2 Corinthians 2:15), like the distinctive taste of a local wine. Have you ever felt envy for someone else's strengths or resources? Jealous of blessings or praise given to others?

It's a natural tendency. Irish playwright Oscar Wilde observed, "anybody can sympathise with the sufferings of a friend, but it requires a very fine nature to sympathise with a friend's success." What should be our perspective & why? How can Christ help us acquire that "very fine nature?" (Hint: John 3:30)

2. (Ch. 2) CS Lewis wrote we are likely chosen by God for tasks because of characteristics different than what we often think. What do you think he meant? Do you agree? Can you think of any examples in your life, acquaintances, or the Bible?

3. (Ch. 3) Read Acts 16:6-10 and James 4:13-15. When you are sincerely following God and an obstacle arises, how do you respond? Give up? Continue along the same path? Listen to God's voice for new direction? How do you deal with change in your life's plans?

4. (Ch. 4) Although living alone and distant from others may shield us from conflict, the highest and most enduring joys also come from living in community, which at its best is "common unity." Modern society is increasingly fragmented and individualistic, and church participation has decreased in recent decades in much of Western culture. Consider the following passages:

Hebrews 10:24-25a: *...let us consider how we may spur one another on toward love and good deeds, not giving up meeting together, as some are in the habit of doing, but encouraging one another...*

1 Corinthians 12:24b-27: *God has put the body together, giving greater honor to the parts that lacked it, so that there should be no division in the body, but that its parts should have equal concern for each other. If one part suffers, every part suffers with it; if one part is honored, every part rejoices with it. Now you are the body of Christ, and each one of you is a part of it.*

Romans 12:4-5,10: *For just as each of us has one body with many members, and these members do not all have the same function, so in Christ we, though many, form one body, and each member belongs to all the others. Be devoted to one another in love. Honor one another above yourselves.*

Galatians 6:2: *Bear one another's burdens, and so fulfill the law of Christ.*

What are some of the reasons you think God instituted the church? He could just as easily created each of us to interact only with him. Part of the answer may be we need to serve each other to develop our souls to better conform to God, who is Love. Doubtlessly, outward-focus service also helps us escape the prison of our own selfish, limited perspective and desires. What else?

What do you think Paul means by "the law of Christ?"

7. (Ch. 5) Are you able to serve in your local Christian community? If not, why not? Have you considered starting a ministry – even if it's just you? Talk with your pastor about your ideas. Something as simple as writing a card once a week to someone others have forgotten can make a tremendous difference!

8. (Ch. 5) Are you more of an introvert or an extrovert? The distinction doesn't depend on how comfortable you feel with others, but more on where you go to recharge your batteries – by yourself or with others. How can your natural disposition help you uniquely serve God?

9. (Ch. 5) In his book *A Severe Mercy*, Sheldon Vanauken shares the difficult experience of his wife's death interpreted (at least by a friend of his) as a pruning event. Although we can't know God's purposes with certainty, Vanauken did grow closer to God afterwards. It may be that some cases of pruning are simply unfortunate circumstances that God did not design, but, from which if we let him, can bring good. Romans 8:28 tells us that "in all things God works for the good for those who love him and are called according to his purpose."

Read Luke 13:1-9. In difficult times, regardless of how we may interpret the circumstances, what actions or attitudes are healthy? Compare those with how Job reacted to his suffering – what are the similarities and differences?

10. (Ch. 6) Cicero once wrote, "gratitude is not only the greatest of virtues, but the parent of virtues."

Goethe penned, "wine rejoices the heart of man and joy is the mother of all virtues."

What is a virtue? Do you agree with Cicero? Goethe? Both? Why or why not?

11. (Ch. 6) John Henry Newman, a 19th century Oxford bishop expanded on another of Cicero's maxims: "Virtue is its own reward, and brings with it the truest and highest pleasure; but if we cultivate it only for pleasure's sake, we are selfish, not religious, and will never gain the pleasure, because we can never have the virtue."

How do we cultivate virtue? If we agree with Cicero that gratitude is the greatest of virtues, how do we cultivate gratitude and joy?

Professional "gratitude experts" recommend keeping a gratitude journal and maintaining friendships with grateful individuals. These same experts have found that this virtue *is* indeed its own reward. Further, they note one of the determinants in how happy you are in life relates how much gratitude you *show*. In other words, happiness tends to increase just by recording gratitude, and rises even higher if you express it to the person responsible!

12. (Ch. 6) What should be the biggest source of gratitude for Christians? How can we express our gratitude? Scientists tell us (see above) that expressing gratitude generally increases joy – is that what you experience? If not, why do you thank that is?

13. (Ch. 6) Jesus says "the kingdom of God isn't here or there but inside you" (Luke 17:21). Sustained joy is something we largely generate as a byproduct seeking goals external to ourselves, not found by self-absorbed pursuit. Three months after a significant life change in circumstances (perceived as either good or bad), most of us settle back to a baseline level of (dis-)satisfaction. What anxieties or fears most often rob us of joy?

14. (Ch. 6) Scientists have also determined that commitment to a decision fosters happiness whereas vacillation typically brings misery. Read I Kings 18:21 and Joshua 24:15. What benefits comes from standing firm in one's faith and committed to God's principles?

14. (Ch. 6) Scottish economist Adam Smith, the intellectual father of capitalism, claimed bounded, not unbounded, ambition leads to contentment. Do you have a primary ambition in your life? What is it?

15. (Ch. 7) In *The Lion, the Witch, and the Wardrobe*, CS Lewis paints a scene where the children anxiously ask

Mr. Beaver about meeting the great Lion. *"'Safe?' said Mr Beaver ... 'Who said anything about safe? Course he isn't safe. But he's good. He's the King, I tell you.'"*

Are there places or events that God has taken you through that initially you feared or resisted but in retrospect were necessary for your growth or blessing? Are there similar areas in your life today? How do you prepare for or deal with them? What can help you make difficult decisions?

16. (Ch. 8) In his letters to fellow believers in Ephesus (Eph. 1:9, 3:3, 3:4, 3:6, 3:9, 5:32, 6:19) and Colossae (Col. 1:26, 1:27, 2:2, 4:3), Paul doesn't shrink away from declaring the gospel as "mystery." Pioneer of the human genome project and Christian, Dr. Francis Collins points out that as expansive as human knowledge is and may become in the future, there will always be material we won't be able to know. There will always be truth beyond the boundaries of our understanding.

In 1603, philosopher, statesman, and developer of the scientific method Sir Francis Bacon wrote, "God hath framed the mind of man as a glass capable of the image of the universal world, joyning to receive the signature thereof as the light is of light, yea not only satisfied in beholding the variety of things and vicissitude of times, but raised also to find out and discern those ordinances and decrees which throughout all these changes are infallibly observed." Bacon and Collins would certainly agree that Christians honor God in committing to learning and teaching truth of all types. When then are we to be content with mystery?

17. (Ch. 8) According to Mahayana Buddhism, the most virtuous beings are Bodhisattvas, compassionate individuals who, rather than enter into Nirvana, stay behind to help others go in first. In contrast, Christ teaches that in blessing others in response to God's love we more deeply experience the joys he intends for us, and the reality of the Kingdom is present before, during, and after those events. Further, paradise has doors God has opened for us, and as we serve, we walk in *with* others, *not* either/or. Can you think of a time serving others brought you blessing when you weren't expecting it?

18. (Ch. 10) Paul encourages his readers to "rejoice and share joy in the same way." What do you think that means? He seems to link service to others with joy. Based on your answers above, do you think the two are related?

19. In this study on the fruit of the vine, we haven't discussed that (1.) some religions outside Christianity forbid alcohol, (2.) there are sincere followers of Christ who drink as well others who strongly believe believers should abstain, and (3.) alcoholism is a tragic disease that affects millions of people worldwide. While there are other New Testaments verses through which we can thoughtfully approach the topic of wine consumption in modern society, consider the two below:

Mark 7:18b-22

"Do you not understand that whatever goes into the man from outside cannot defile him, because it does not go into his heart, but into his stomach, and is eliminated?" (Thus He declared all foods clean.) And He was saying, "That which proceeds out of the man, that is what defiles the man. For from within, out of the heart of men, proceed the evil thoughts, fornications, thefts, murders, adulteries, deeds of coveting and wickedness, as well as deceit, sensuality, envy, slander, pride and foolishness."

I Corinthians 8: 8-13

Food will not commend us to God; we are neither the worse if we do not eat, nor the better if we do eat. But take care that this liberty of yours does not somehow become a stumbling block to the weak. For if someone sees you, who have knowledge, dining in an idol's temple, will not his conscience, if he is weak, be strengthened to eat things sacrificed to idols? For through your knowledge he who is weak is ruined, the brother for whose sake Christ died. And so, by sinning against the brethren and wounding their conscience when it is weak, you sin against Christ. Therefore, if food causes my brother to stumble, I will never eat meat again, so that I will not cause my brother to stumble.

What general principles do you take from these passages (or others)?

20. Which lesson in this study has moved you most strongly to love better? Which has helped you build others up more effectively? Apply them today, and may God bless you as you pour your life into others!

I Corinthians 8: 1b:
Knowledge makes arrogant, but love edifies.

§

Psalm 4:7
*You have put gladness in my heart,
More than when their grain and new wine abound.*

www.ingramcontent.com/pod-product-compliance
Lightning Source LLC
Chambersburg PA
CBHW060820050426
42449CB00008B/1743